101 Ways to Know . . . It's Time to Leave Your Mama's House

Also by the Wayans Brothers

101 Ways to Know You're a Golddigger
101 Ways to Know You're Having a Ghetto Christmas

101
ways to know . . .
it's time to leave your mama's house

Keenen Ivory Wayans,
Shawn Wayans,
Marlon Wayans,
and Shane Miller

St. Martin's Griffin 🅜 New York

Waldorf West Branch
10405 O'Donnell Place
Waldorf, MD 20603

www.stmartins.com

Library of Congress Cataloging-in-Publication Data

Wayans, Keenen Ivory.
    101 ways to know it's time to leave your mama's house/keenen, Shawn, and Marlon Wayans.—1st ed.
        p. cm.
    ISBN-13: 978-0312-35968-3
    ISBN-10: 0-312-35968-3
    1. Mothers—Humor. 2. Adult children living with parents—Humor. I. Wayans, Shawn, 1971-II. Wayans, Marlon. III. Title.
    PN6231.M68A35 2009
    818'.5402—dc22

                                                                    2009004806

First Edition: May 2009

P 1

To our parents, for raising us to be responsible Mama's house men and women; and even though all their actions said get the hell out of my house, they never actually said it.
So, thank you Mom and Pop; we love you.

And to our kids: We love you, thanks for being our inspiration, and when you turn 18, GET OUT!

Acknowledgments

Thank you to our family, all 9 million of them.
And to our team: Rick Alvarez, Lisa Bloom, Mike Tidded,
Luom Cooper, Coral Compagnono, and Danielle Casinelli.
Special thanks to Shane Miller, Darren Huang,
Layron Dejarnette, and David Torres.
Thank you all for your contributions.

101 Ways to Know . . . It's Time to Leave Your Mama's House

You know it's time to leave your mama's house if . . .

You catch your mama having sex on the living room couch.

**Your mama decides to vacuum
while you're in the middle of reading a book.**

Your mama has your car towed.

You catch your mama using your razor to shave her privates.

Your mama yells at you for keeping the toilet seat up.

Your mama still sends you out to buy her personal hygiene products.

Your mama hogs the TV so much that now
Lifetime is your favorite channel.

You have to wash the dishes but you didn't even eat.

Your mama catches you masturbating.

Your mama turns your room into her gym.

Your mama uses all the hot water.

You have to sneak girls in.

Your mama entertains your date with embarrassing pictures of you as a kid.

Your mama still opens your mail.

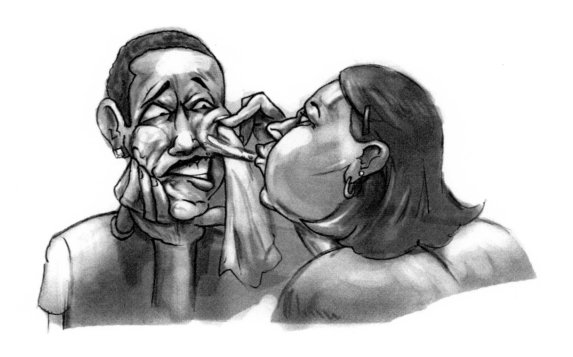

Your mama still washes your face with spit.

Your mama changes the locks after you turn eighteen.

Your mama smokes up all your weed.

You have to pay admission in order to get in the house.

Your mama installs a pay phone.

Your mama walks around the house naked when you have company over.

Your mama interrupts your phone sex.

The IRS audits you because your mama still claims you on her taxes.

Your mama is always trying to hook you up with a "good" woman.

Your mama goes through your stuff.

Your mama kicks you out of your room to accommodate her boyfriend's friends.

Your mama has you arrested for home invasion.

Your mama gives you a two-hour financial seminar every time you ask for money.

Your mama hires a witch doctor to get you out of the house.

You have to be on the guest list in order to get in the house.

PETITION

We, the undersigned, have been informed that Craig "Sugar" Jackson has been living with his mama for the last thirty years. He is a no good for nothing child trapped in a man's body. We urge you to have Sugar Jackson get the hell out of his mama's house and find his own damn place!

NAME	SIGNATURE	RELATION
TOMIKA J.	*signature*	MAMA
James J	*signature*	POP
Sheena C	*signature*	SISTER
PHIL WILLIAMS	*signature*	DUDE DOWN THE STREET
MIKE T.	*signature*	YOU OWE ME 10 BUCKS SUGAR
ED .	*signature*	GRANDMA
YOU SUCK	CRAIG GET	OUT YOU
PEICE OF	CRAP .	
DAN GARCIA	*signature*	EX - FRIEND
STACY ALLEN	*signature*	EX - GIRLFRIEND
BRIAN VAN	*signature*	MAIL MAN
ROBERT	*signature*	BUMM
Pete James	*signature*	BRO
ANAYE	*signature*	NEIGHBOR
TOM KELER	*signature*	TRASH MAN
LIZ BERGER	*signature*	12th GRADE TEACHER
TOMIKA J.	*signature*	MAMA
TAMIKA J.	*signature*	MAMA
STAN G	*signature*	LANDLORD
	paw print	

Everyone in your house signed a petition asking you to move out.

Your mama calls you at work to tell you to clean your room.

Your mama moved and didn't tell you.

You found the movie *Baby Boy* "deep."

Your mama makes you the plumber, gardener, and the maid.

Your mama refers to you as "That Lazy Motha!@$#!"

You get a bill after breakfast.

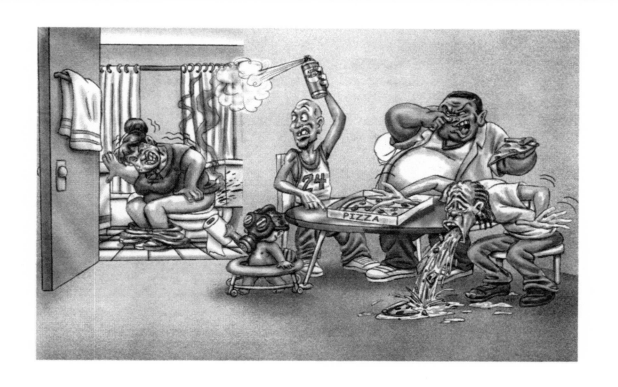

Your mama takes a shit with the door open.

Your mama's always hitting on your friends.

Your mama sets up booby traps outside your door.

Your mama's boyfriend wears your clothes.

Your mama wires your car to explode.

Your mama gives you the finger every time you leave the house.

You think the bum living in a cardboard box got his shit together.

Your mama tries to suffocate you while you're sleeping.

Your mama cuts you out of the family pictures.

Your mama treats the dog better than you.

If the welcome mat reads "FUCK OFF, SON."

Your mama taxes your check.

Your mama calls in bomb threats to get you out of the house.

Your mama taped over your favorite movie with homemade porn.

Your mama got you luggage, an apartment guide,
and a U-Haul truck for Christmas.

Your mama fumigates the house while you're in it.

Your mama starts to renovate the house while you're still in it.

Your mama has to have lawyers present when you borrow money.

Your mama puts a three-day eviction notice on your door.

You're waiting for your mama to die so you can take over the lease.

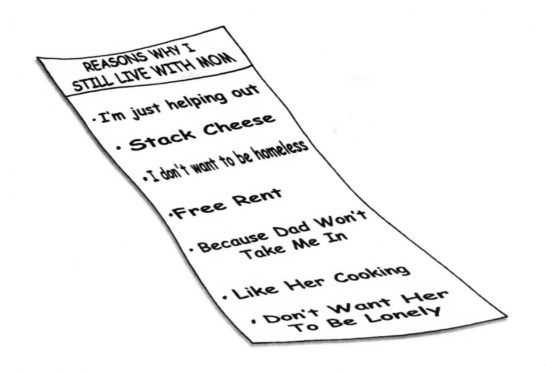

REASONS WHY I STILL LIVE WITH MOM

- I'm just helping out
- Stack Cheese
- I don't want to be homeless
- Free Rent
- Because Dad Won't Take Me In
- Like Her Cooking
- Don't Want Her To Be Lonely

You use the excuse "I'm just helping Mom out."

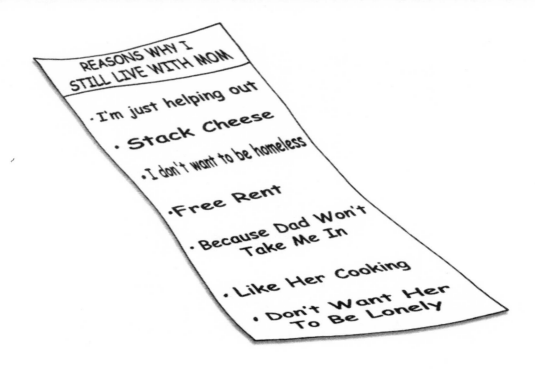

REASONS WHY I STILL LIVE WITH MOM

- I'm just helping out
- Stack Cheese
- I don't want to be homeless
- Free Rent
- Because Dad Won't Take Me In
- Like Her Cooking
- Don't Want Her To Be Lonely

You use the excuse "I'm just living with my mom so I can stack some cheese."

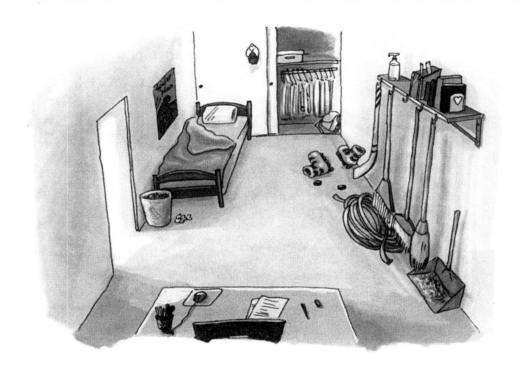

Your room doubles as a broom closet.

Your mama asks, "When are you moving out?" and your grandmother asks her, "When are you moving out?"

Your mama haunts the house just to get you the hell out.

Your mama becomes allergic to you.

MARY WILLIAMS
LA MAR WILLIAMS
5436 BAKER ST.
COMPTON, CA 90020

101

MAY 20 08

PAY TO THE ORDER OF _Wall Mart_

16.89

Sixteen + 89/100 _____ DOLLARS

BANK OF MISTRUST
P.O. BOX 63304, 464 SLAUSON AVENUE, CALIFORNIA 90220

MEMO _Soulja Boy CD_   SIGNED _LaMar Williams_

You have a joint account with your mama.

Your mama hangs up a long list of things she hates about you.

Your mama calls CSI to see if you had sex in her bed.

Your mama calls immigration to have you deported.

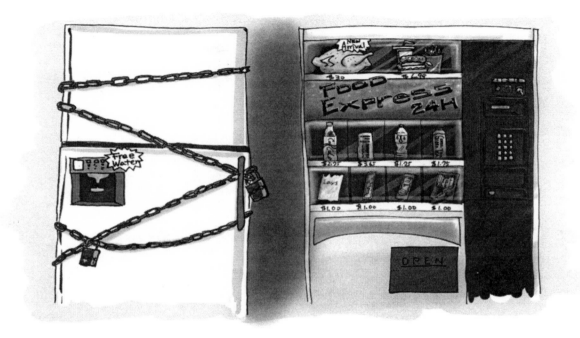

Your mama replaces your refrigerator with a vending machine.

Your mama charges for everything you take from the fridge.

You're the only one not invited to your birthday party.

Your mama and her new boyfriend use up all your condoms.

Your mama enlists you in the army.

Your mama fakes her own death in order to get you out.

Nobody in the house respects your privacy.

There's a fire in the house and your room is the only one that burns down.

Your mama decides to watch a televangelist on Super Bowl Sunday.

Your mama uses your room for storage space.

Your mama tries to frame you for a third strike.

Your mama uses your room as a homeless shelter.

Your mama lets your creditors know that you're home.

Your mama sells her sold to the devil to get you out of the house.

Your mama makes a dartboard out of your baby pictures.

Your prolonged presence has made your mama pro-choice.

Your mama hangs her douche bag outside of your window.

Your mama cusses out everyone who calls for you.

Your mama gains access to your MySpace account and puts herself in your top eight.

Your mama celebrates every time you leave the house.

Your mama introduces you to strangers who are looking for roommates.

Your mama cooks for everybody in the house except you.

Your mama hides all the food.

Your mama prays to get you out of her house.

Your mama smokes only in your room.

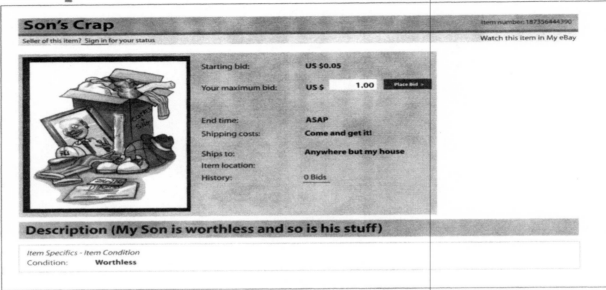

Your mama sells all your belongings on eBay.

If she puts a "room for rent" sign on the lawn.

Your mama uses your bedroom to host her bridge night.

Your mama makes your wallpaper out of "apartment for lease" ads.

You have a wife and kids, and you're
still living under your mama's roof.

Your mama buys a pit bull and trains it to bark only at you.

You and your mama fight over the same parking space.

Your mama lets Osama Bin Laden hide out in your room.

Your mama's only birthday wish was for you to get out.

If reading this book brought tears to your eyes.